# RUBES

## BIBLE
### CARTOONS

# Leigh Rubin

HENDRICKSON
PUBLISHERS

How did I get started doing Bible cartoons? Well, take one doodling, daydreaming kid with a short attention span and sit him down in a Sunday School class. What do you get? It may not be quite the stuff that Biblical scholars are made of, but it did provide the early inspiration for what later became one of my favorite topics as a syndicated cartoonist.

Who isn't fascinated by those ancient celebrities of the Bible—Adam and Eve, Noah, Moses, and Jonah? We all know their stories. But when I think of these larger-than-life characters I can't help asking, "What if?" What if the Red Sea had not parted—did Moses have a Plan B? What if Noah had been paid off by the beef industry? What would Adam have done to impress Eve? What would it have been like for Methuselah to outlive all his contemporaries? What if Jonah had been a member of Greenpeace?

Then there are those spectacular Biblical events! Could there be a hidden reason why it took Moses and company forty years to cross the wilderness? How did David overcome Goliath's tremendous home court advantage? How did the animals that didn't make it onto Noah's Ark feel about being left behind?

It's questions like these that still inspire me to daydream and doodle.

Leigh Rubin

## Dedication

To my sons—Jeremy, Ryan, and Andrew

Each of you is an inspiration.

**In an attempt to impress the girl,
Adam shows off his family tree.**

**Daniel enters the Lion's Den.**

**Methuselah's editor**

**A.D. 79: Mount Vesuvius spells disaster for Pompeii, not to mention Julian's novelty business.**

**Moses pens his personal ad.**

"I don't mean to rush you, old boy,
but would you mind deciphering those
hieroglyphs a bit faster? . . . I urgently
need to use the lavatory!"

**Adam receives the first indication that all is not perfect in paradise.**

5-15

"I understand the need for our religion to
change with the times, but personally,
I prefer a more traditional burnt offering."

"Offhand, I'd say we're
somewhere in the Sinai Desert."

At 3 hours, 29 minutes and 10 seconds,
young Moses achieves his
personal best at the 100 meters.

"Look on the bright side. Since this is
a religious contribution, your donation
is completely tax-deductible."

"Congratulations, Bob, you made it!
Just watch your step. . . . As I'm sure you've
heard by now, all dogs go to heaven."

At an emergency meeting of the
Idol Makers' Association

**Another disappointing birthday
in the Sahara**

**Quite popular among Roman children was helmet night at the Coliseum.**

"OK, everybody, stay back.
There's a car coming!"

"Next time, I suggest you leave
the beavers at home."

**ATMs before cash**

"We just booked some punk with a sling
down at the station. . . . He claims
it was self-defense."

"I can't believe you missed the Canaan exit!
The next one isn't for forty years!"

**Knowing full well he would never have to pay a single claim, Noah cleans up.**

**In Moses' mother's kitchen**

- 32 -

**If Moses came down from
the mountain today**

"I'm all for having children, Eve, but even just one kid would increase the Earth's population by 50 percent!"

**Methuselah, frequent target of
Old Testament tongue-wagging**

"Excuse me, sir, but I believe you were supposed to lead us to the land of milk *and* honey?"

Moses wisely leaves nothing to chance.

**Omar made the tragic mistake of overdoing it at the Pharaoh's tomb-sealing party.**

**Troublemaker in paradise.**

"Tut is a mummy's boy!
Tut is a mummy's boy!"

**Less permanent but equally impressive were the other Egyptian pyramids.**

"Five o'clock . . . Time to wrap it up."

**Jobs versus progress circa 1455.**

**"Excellent! Pharaoh will be quite pleased to learn that you've completed construction under budget and ahead of schedule."**

**Adam and Eve's hamper**

**God's factory seconds**

"I can't believe it . . . here we are, living in eternal paradise, and all *you* can do is complain that the mattress is too soft!"

**The reason it took forty years**

"I'm sorry, God, but I'm afraid this has so many problems that it's beyond repair. I suggest you toss it and create a new one."

**Fire ignited by a bolt of lighting completely gutted the atheist's meeting hall. Sadly, their insurance policy did not cover acts of God.**

**Moses almost blows the job interview.**

**Despite months of careful planning,
Noah overlooked one small detail.**

"With all due respect, oh Greatest of High Priests, I believe that the 50 percent drop in attendance at our worship services can be directly attributed to the fact that you've sacrificed half the congregation."

"Better hold up on the sacrifice . . .
I'm having serious thoughts about
changing my religious affiliation."

**Noah's plan to save the animals runs into opposition from another environmental interest group.**

**Though he held a prestigious and respected position, the royal scribe had little time to enjoy his official status as he was always trying to catch up on the never-ending mountain of papyrus work.**

**"Absolutely not, Noah!
You may not keep them!"**

"Bad news, folks . . . one of us has to
go back to the land of bondage
and get some lighter fluid."

**Moses: advertising wiz**

**Moses' kid**

**Before Tupperware, there were earthenware parties.**

**Why Adam *really* wanted a mate**

**Hardest hit by the departure of Moses and company were the slave drivers.**

**Moses hangs ten across the Red Sea.**

WHILE FAITH AND HUMILITY WERE INDEED VALUED, THE MONASTERY'S RESTROOM SHORTAGE WAS A CONSTANT REMINDER THAT THE MOST IMPORTANT VIRTUE OF ALL WAS PATIENCE.

MIRACULOUSLY, THE DEFENSE PARTED AND MOSES DELIVERED

**Mummy hampers**

**Ancient Egyptians took great care in
providing a comfortable after-life for
their beloved Pharaoh by selecting
food that would last an eternity.**

"Unbelievable! Another outrageous
heating bill!"

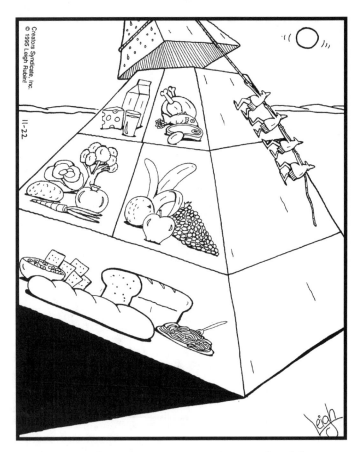

**Health-conscious Egyptians build the great food guide pyramid.**

"Gentlemen, I have reason to believe
that there's an imposter among us."

**Quite possibly the least utilized
service in hell**

**Methuselah, the smart shopper**

**Biblical insider trading**

**Ray was unaware that
"certain restrictions" applied.**

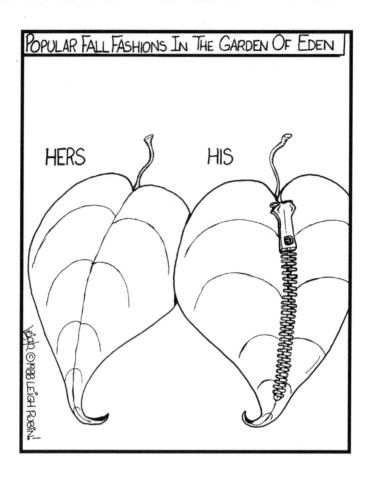

**With just one rest room on board, this would be only the first of many lines.**

**There was only one way for David to overcome Goliath's tremendous home court advantage.**

**In his haste to beat the inclement weather,
Noah overlooked one small detail.**

**Moses departs on his flight from
the land of bondage.**

**There were a few who felt a strong need to express their opinions at being left behind.**

"Think how much easier this job would be
if we could just stuff these stiffs
into Tupperware!"

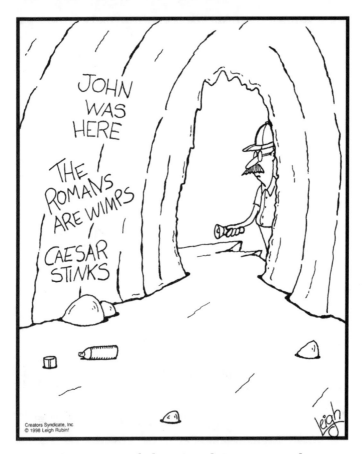

**Discovery of the Dead Sea Scrawls.**

Perhaps even more depressing than
watching the weather channel in hell
was the fact that it was the
*only* channel in hell.

"If I told you once, I told you a hundred
times . . . patience is a virtue,
you little twit!"

**Darkness descended upon the land. It was time to put the sphinx out for the night.**

" . . . There were thousands of 'em, all clamoring to get on board, but I only had room for two of each. So I thought to myself, 'It sure would be a shame for all of those magnificent creatures to go to waste.'"

**"It may not be one of the Seven Wonders of the World, but it's certainly going to do wonders for our tourist industry."**

**Methuselah at his two-hundredth
high school reunion**

"Doesn't Thog look silly?! He must not know
that *our* pile of rocks is the *real* God!"

"My phone number? You've gotta be kidding! Why, I don't know you from Adam!"

"I'm a little short on cash. Can
I pay ya next week?"

**Ultimately, it was the vow of celibacy that convinced Harold to seek another line of work.**

**If Noah were paid off by the beef industry**

"Say, Brutus, it suddenly occurred to me that if we leave now, we can beat the crowds."

"Why, of course you're welcome to join our monastery. I'm quite certain that you'll make an excellent fryer."

"Be careful with that thing, David.
You could hurt someone!"

**Methuselah made his psychiatrist
a very wealthy man.**

**A blessing in disguise**

**Just in case the water failed to part,
there was always "Plan B."**

**Calendars in hell**

**Although he was a devout believer
in creation, there were times when
evolution seemed quite plausible.**

"Listen, Noah, I gotta run. The basement's
getting flooded. Have a nice time
on your cruise!"

**To help pass time on the long journey, Moses often listened to scrolls on tape.**

**Goliath's final diary entry**

**"What a lousy trip . . . it rained
the *whole time!*"**

**Omar was spared serious injury thanks to his driver's side air bag.**

"I've got a bad feeling about this."

**God plays connect-the-dots.**

**Cow hell**

**Samson's plan hits a snag.**

**The first ever after-Christmas sale**

**Unbeknownst to most biblical scholars, there were actually three cows on board Noah's Ark.**

**Brother Dominick makes his first
and last talk show appearance.**

**Classic example of management
being out of touch with labor**